A Blended
FAMILY

BASED ON A TRUE STORY

Roy Mamah

A Blended Family

Table of Contents

DEDICATION

This book is lovingly dedicated to my mother, Elone Julie Senge, who taught me the valuable lessons of patience, love, and forgiveness.

Despite experiencing the challenges of being in a blended family herself, she never passed on the pain or bitterness to me. Instead, she showed me how to embrace love, understanding, and acceptance. Her selflessness and grace have been a constant source of inspiration to me, and I strive to follow in her footsteps.

I also dedicate this book to my children, who have shown remarkable love, acceptance, and inclusivity towards their siblings, Alice and Lahar, despite knowing they are their half-siblings. My boys, Aldrin, Vahid and Jaden your unwavering support and bond with one another is a proof of the power of love and the beauty of blended families.

PREFACE

In a world where relationships and families are as diverse as the people who form them, *A Blended Family* unveils the intricate curtains of love, challenges, and triumphs that arise when hearts and lives intertwine. This book offers a compassionate and insightful exploration of the complexities I faced in my blended family. These families are formed when individuals bring together their children from previous relationships. Through heartfelt narratives and real-life examples, you will discover the resilient bonds that were formed as my family navigated the uncharted waters of shared homes, shared dreams, and shared love.

FORWARD

My first encounter with the author of this great piece of art was virtually, yet every moment I listened or read her, it sounded anew. Germaine (Roy Mamah) does not only get you to feel her, she takes you along in a less complicated but enriching healing process. One of the areas of her works that got me blended with her, is her proclivity towards youth empowerment and development.

I would not have imagined myself amongst the numerous experts in relationship stories to be the one to Foreword A Blended Family. The relationship coach and motivational speaker, I should say par excellence, has once more beaten many in the trade by going this far. Roy Mamah makes me jealous of this modern family paradigm which embodies a powerful testament to the strength of love, adaptability and unity - *A Blended Family.*

Explaining how these families showcase the remarkable capacity of human beings to embrace change, cultivate connections and build nurturing environments that foster the well-being of every member completely got me involved. I may not have direct or immediate blended family experiences, but I think I now understand why in the later years of my Father's life, he always told me that a child is a child, no matter who gave birth to that child. I can't explain further.

A Blended Family? Yes – She takes her time, presenting stories of her personal experiences on how she navigates new roles, builds connections towards her first love to co and transitional parenting, blending family dynamics, towards love without boundaries, honoring individualities, navigating complexities and creating a lasting legacy, in a subtle manner that will make you feel part of the reading journey.

As I encourage you to read and read this piece all over again, bear with me that it is truly an odyssey of comprehension and reverence-a pilgrimage to unearth the profound strength that binds blended families together.

By Barrister Felix Nkongho Agbor- Balla

INTRODUCTION

In today's diverse and evolving world, families come in a wide array of shapes and sizes, reflecting the unique stories and journeys of each individual. Among these dynamic family structures, the concept of *Blended Families* has risen to prominence, showcasing its prevalence and remarkable impact.

A Blended Family, also known as a stepfamily or reconstituted family, emerges when two individuals in a new relationship bring with them children from previous marriages or relationships. This fusion of lives and experiences results in the formation of a fresh family unit, wherein the new couple collaborates to nurture and support their children, both biological and stepchildren alike.

This modern family paradigm embodies a powerful testament to the strength of love, adaptability, and unity. Blended Families challenge traditional norms and assumptions, illustrating that the bonds of kinship extend beyond biological connections. The journey of a blended family is one characterized by growth, understanding, and the merging of individual narratives into a collective story of resilience and harmony.

As Blended Families continue to thrive and redefine the boundaries of family dynamics, they exemplify the potential for love and compassion to transcend challenges and complexities. These families showcase the remarkable capacity of human beings to embrace change, cultivate connections, and build nurturing environments that foster the well-being of every member.

The existence and flourishing of Blended Families in our society underscore the richness of human relationships and the boundless capacity of the heart to expand its embrace. With each day, these families rewrite the script of traditional family structures, reminding us all that love knows no limits and that the blending of lives can create a scene of remarkable strength and enduring unity.

Blended families can take various forms, depending on the circumstances and relationships involved. Some common scenarios include:

1. Stepfamily

When one partner has children from a previous marriage or relationship, and the other partner does not have any biological children.

2. Step-siblings

When both partners have children from previous relationships, and they bring their respective children together to form a larger stepfamily.

3. Half-siblings

When a couple has children together in their current marriage or relationship, and each parent also has children from previous relationships.

Navigating the intricate paths of blending families is a journey fraught with challenges, for it involves intertwining lives shaped by diverse backgrounds, experiences, and family dynamics. In the heart of this complex endeavor lies the vital triumvirate of communication, understanding, and patience—a trio that serves as a guiding compass through the complications of blended family dynamics. While the road may be arduous, the destination promises the creation of an avenue woven with strong bonds and unwavering love, a testament to the unyielding dedication of each family member to cultivate a harmonious and nurturing environment.

Within the realm of A Blended Family, we shall embark on an exploration that unveils the complexity and nuances that render these families truly remarkable. By delving deep into the dynamics, we will glean insights into the valuable life lessons they bestow upon them. Drawing inspiration from a real-life story and personal anecdotes, we shall bear witness to the extraordinary resilience and unwavering commitment that characterizes these family unions.

As we venture forth, we shall trace the footprints of our families, tracing our steps as they navigate the complexities of our pasts. Through shared experiences, we shall uncover the mechanisms that enable us to forge pathways towards unity, understanding and affection. Our journey is an odyssey of comprehension and reverence, a pilgrimage to unearth the profound strength that binds blended families together.

Amidst the complexity of blended families, let us revel in our uniqueness and cherish the insights I offer. This is an expedition that promises a deepened appreciation for the intricate web of relationships woven within our families and society today. As we walk hand in hand with our stories, we shall come to realize that the power of a blended family lies not just in our ability to navigate challenges, but in our ability to foster a love that transcends the boundaries of tradition and creates a mosaic of connection and support.

Chapter 1
BEGINNINGS & BONDS

In the heart of West Africa, beneath the golden sun and the gentle sway of Cameroon's lush landscapes, a story of family, love, and transformation unfolds. Born into a family of five and nestled within the embrace of a tranquil southern village. We were a portrait of the quintessential family, I believed in my innocent youth. With my mother, father, elder brother, and younger sister, we formed a harmonious unit, admired and respected by our neighbors. My father, a dedicated servant in the military's secret service, and my mother, a diligent government school teacher, painted a picture of love and stability.

As a young girl, I held my father close to my heart, oblivious to the complexities of the world around me. Our evenings were sacred, an oasis of unity and warmth, as my father would return home, ensuring we prayed together and shared precious moments before bedtime. The highlight of my school days was the sight of my father's smile upon my return, a smile that held the power to infuse my heart with joy and love. His embrace, his kisses, they cocooned me in a sense of safety and belonging. May his soul rest in peace.

In those days, my parents were inseparable, their love an unbreakable bond. Laughter echoed through our home, and the memories of blissful vacations lingered in the corridors of my mind. Yet, amidst this idyllic setting, there was a shadow, a perplexing and painful aspect of their relationship, the occasional disputes that would flare into storms. These quarrels would escalate until my mother, overwhelmed, would depart for extended periods of time, leaving us with an aching void. As a tender child, I couldn't fathom the reasons behind her departures, and it left me bewildered. Only with the passage of time did I begin to discern the heart-wrenching truth: my mother was enduring physical abuse. She kept that a secret for the longest until I found a picture of her bruised face and confronted her. Yet she protected him by saying good tidings.

During these tumultuous times, my father would whisk us away to our grandmother's home, seeking respite from the anguish that plagued their relationship. In our tight-knit community, such matters were shrouded in secrecy, and the voices of children held no sway in the decisions of adults. We were left to grapple with our emotions, unable to articulate our fears and concerns. Yet, my father, despite the challenges, rose to the occasion, assuming the roles of both parents.

He accompanied us to school, prepared our meals, and did his utmost to fill the void left by my mother's absence. Though I yearned for her presence, I adapted to this new reality as the seasons passed. Her eventual return was always a ray of hope, and during her absence, my father labored tirelessly to ensure we felt loved and cared for. Through this tumultuous journey, we gleaned the profound importance of open communication and empathy within a family. Armed with love, patience, and understanding, we ventured forth, cherishing the moments of beauty while confronting life's formidable challenges.

Once upon a time, our neighbors would gaze upon the attractive sight of my parents and me strolling hand in hand down our community's cobblestone streets, sharing in the bonds of family. But those memories now lay distant, fading like the twilight into night. There came a pivotal juncture when my dad made a fateful decision to introduce a second wife into our family. In my tender innocence, I Couldn't fathom the implications of this choice, and the anticipation that had danced in my heart was not met with joy.

With my mother absent during this transformation, the arrival of this elegant woman didn't fill me with excitement as I had once envisioned danger. Instead, I longed for the days of vacations, yearning to reunite with my mother. Alas, fate unfurled a different setting, and this beautiful lady assumed her place within our home, bearing the title of a "Mother." As the sands of time drifted on, we endeavored to accept her as our second mom, but the tides of change were not in our favor. At an age when I should have been preoccupied with childhood whimsies, I found myself burdened with the responsibilities of adulthood, washing dishes, cooking meals, and tending to the household's demands.

It was a weight I couldn't bear, and the rationale behind these shifts remained a mystery. I believed it to be the normal course for young women, an inexorable part of the journey into adulthood. The ember of hope, that one day I would reside with my mother again, flickered relentlessly. Yet, the cruel twist of fate would not grant me that wish. This phase of my life marked an irrevocable shift, thrusting me into a maelstrom of challenges that I could not fully comprehend, challenges that would shape my emotional well-being and development.

The arrival of a second wife reshaped the very essence of our family dynamics, and I found myself struggling to contain the enigma unfolding before me. This is how my blended family started.

Chapter 2
NAVIGATING NEW ROLES

In the recesses of my memories, my kid sister, the echoes of our shared past resurface like fragments of a distant dream. A particular incident, shrouded in the mists of time, when she, at a tender age, around ten, grappled with the unsettling ordeal of bedwetting. Her distress at this nocturnal occurrence remains etched in my mind.

I can vividly summon the image of us being gently lifted from our beds, our soft sanctuary, and deposited onto the hard, unforgiving floor. This transition bore an air of solemnity, tinged with unspoken concern, a ritual that unfolded in the silence of the night. Furthermore, etched in the parchment of my memory are the recollections of those times when we faced discipline and punishment in the wake of such bedwetting incidents.

These experiences left indelible marks upon my soul, forging a path of understanding and empathy. I began to shoulder the responsibilities that were assigned to my sister, seeking to alleviate her distress and the torrents of tears that threatened to drown her. In my innocence, I believed this was the way of the world, unaware of the true reasons behind my mother's absence. At a tender age I saw myself cooking a big meal then going to bed with an empty stomach because I was refused the same meal I prepared, we were not allowed to tell my dad the ordeals we were facing or else death threats.

Gradually, I became conscious of the chasm that had torn my family asunder. My mother was no longer a presence in our home, replaced by another woman whose true nature remained concealed from my father. My sister and I were shackled by silence, forbidden to utter a single word about the unfolding secrets that threatened our well-being. Menacing shadows of reprisal, hunger, and harm loomed over us, casting a perpetual pall of fear during those tender years.

Time, a relentless river, carried us to new shores. We found ourselves uprooted from the rural landscapes that had cradled our childhood and deposited into an unfamiliar urban terrain. The transition was marked by stark differences, a metamorphosis that demanded adaptation. Yet, within my heart, I retained the spirit of playfulness that defined my youth. Soccer, dodgeball, and carefree escapades with friends provided solace as I navigated these unfamiliar areas. I was but a small-town girl grappling with the complicated alleyways of an urban world.

Amidst this sea of change, a constant beacon illuminated my life every Sunday, the resounding sounds of laughter and song. I had ventured into the church choir, and the intoxication of music and camaraderie became an integral part of my existence.

On Sundays, though, the journey to church was often paved with tears. You could see, I bored the weight of completing a multitude of chores before setting foot inside the sanctuary. Rising at the break of dawn, around 5 a.m., I would diligently toil to prepare everything for the day's activities. On the occasions when I faltered, and the minutes slipped through my fingers, the pressure bore down on me, crushing my spirit. Tears would flow, for my heart yearned to be in church, to lend my voice to the choir and sing with boundless joy.

One fateful day, my father, an early riser and a devotee of soccer games, returned home to find me ensnared in my own tears. He inquired about the source of my anguish, and I poured out my heart, explaining my struggle to complete my tasks before attending church services.

This revelation catalyzed a heated confrontation between my stepmother and my dad, a tempest of frustration and tension.

Amidst the emotional stormy exchange, I sought refuge in the cocoon of my room, my dreams of church going and the choir slipping through my fingers like sand. My stepmother decreed that I would not attend church that day, instructing me to complete my chores with the promise of attendance the following Sunday. It was at that moment when my aspirations collided with the relentless demands of reality, a clash of dreams and daily life.

In those days, school became my sanctuary, the pillar upon which I rested my hopes. My daily routine entailed a fifteen-mile journey on foot to reach my school, a trek that, despite its distance, was an adventure in camaraderie. Walking with friends and classmates, we would gather more companions along the way, transforming the arduous journey into an experience of laughter, stories, and shared experiences. It was a bright contrast to the challenges I faced within my blended family.

During that period, my stepmother introduced her own son and daughter into our lives, bringing with them a web of complexities and adjustments. It was a time when I yearned for affection, especially in the absence of my mother's comforting presence. The maternal care that a young girl seeks eluded my grasp. Yet, in the presence of my father, there was a semblance of a different reality, a glimmer of warmth amid the shadows.

In my treasure trove of memories, one incident remains vivid—a clandestine visit from my mother to our school. She arrived bearing gifts, a large bag filled with tokens of love. However, upon our return home, my brother inadvertently revealed her visit to my stepmother. Tensions soared within the confines of our home. My omission of informing her about my mother's visit was deemed an offence, and the consequence was grievous. I endured severe beatings and was denied access to food for several days.

In a heart-wrenching twist, my stepmother claimed the gifts meant for us and bestowed them upon her own children. The message was clear, and the threat of dire consequences hung heavy in the air. The revelation left me bewildered, shaken to the core by the depth of secrecy and fear that had infiltrated our lives.

Chapter 3
BUILDING CONNECTIONS

L ife, that ever-untamed journey, unfolded its uncertain nature before us, setting our course on an unforeseen trajectory. The catalyst for this transformation was the distressing departure of my step-sister, a moment that carved a profound alteration in the scene of our family's dynamics.

My stepmother, who entered the union bearing a daughter and a son, my father, who brought his own daughters and son into this family fusion. To harmonies our family bonds, the surnames of my step-brother and step-sister were gently reshaped to align with ours. Yet, the true combination of our hearts and lives remained a far more complicated affair.

As the relentless march of time swept us along, the conflicting winds of circumstance grew increasingly turbulent. It was during these difficult days that I, driven by a fierce resolve, made a daring choice, one that would lead me on a solitary path toward the unknown. "My destination" The sprawling city where my mother had once dwelled, a place where I hoped to rediscover solace in the embrace of her presence.

For a week, I existed in a state of uncertainty, a shadow among unfamiliar surroundings, severed from the comforts of my customary existence. Then, like a drifting vessel finally making landfall, I reached out to my father, my voice trembling with emotion, tears pouring out like unspoken anguish that had long boiled within my heart.

Returning home, I confronted a sobering truth: the ideal vision of a harmonious blended family I had yearned for had become an unattainable illusion. The memories that should have been bathed in warmth and affection had been veiled by a disarray of hurt, resentment, and a gaping void of love lessness and communication barriers that spanned the gap between my stepmother and my mother.

The complexities of our situation loomed like towering peaks, casting their shadows over any trace of unity. In those chaotic times, the intangible area of understanding and genuine affection remained just beyond our grasp, a distant dream.

In retrospect, as the wisdom of years unfolded before me like a scene woven from the threads of time, I began to discern the complex web of motivations and choices that had guided our family's course. One thing, however, remained steadfast amidst the shifting sands of our lives: a bond, unbreakable and profound, shared between my step-brother, my step-sister, and myself.

During that turbulent period, the distinctions that adults might perceive among us as children held little influence in our eyes. Despite the occasional whispers of discrimination that brushed against our souls, we forged ahead, united by the unspoken understanding of our shared experiences...

As the hands of time continued their ceaseless journey, I blossomed into a young woman, my heart awakening to the tantalizing allure of love's embrace. High school years ushered in new aspirations, and I made a resolute decision I could no longer reside under my father's roof. This proclamation, delivered with the unwavering clarity of youth, set in motion a chain of events that would unveil unforeseen revelations.

To my surprise, it was my stepmother who played a peculiar role in transporting me to my mother's home. As we arrived at the footsteps of my mother's house, the smell of her delicious meal in preparation floated through the air, signaling an encounter filled with tension. She served us and watched us savor that meal with tension. After we had finished eating, my mother posed a question to my stepmother if she enjoyed her food, to which she replied with courtesy, praising the flavors that danced on her palate. My mother's retort, tinged with a hint of sarcasm altered the course of our interaction. She asked whether my stepmother enjoyed her meals, knowing that her own daughter went hungry in her home, often having to rely on leftovers and occasionally going to bed on an empty stomach. I had explained to my mother prior to our coming, how I always had to ensure everyone else ate and was satisfied before I could even think about having my own meal, and sometimes I had to wait for my dad to come home before I could have a proper meal from his share. The atmosphere grew thick with unspoken grievances and unbridled emotions as they engaged in a dialogue, dissecting various facets of my existence.

The meal, a symbolic battleground, bore witness to their exchange, culminating in my stepmother's eventual departure, a conclusion that marked the dissolution of our strained discourse. The echoes of that encounter would linger, a haunting refrain in the cacophony of my blended family's history.

Chapter 4
MY FIRST SEED

As the sands of time drifted steadily onward, a pivotal moment materialized in my life, a moment of choice that would engrave a profound mark upon my journey. It was my mother who, with a blend of hope and determination, decided to enroll me into a boarding school nestled within the bustling heart of the city. This decision, cloaked in anticipation and optimism, heralded a new chapter brimming with excitement and promises.

High school years in the city unfolded like a colorful quilt, stitched with moments of discovery and opportunities. It was during this changing time that I had the privilege of meeting an exceptional young man, a random meeting that would become an integral part of my life. He came to the city to mark a special event, a celebration that remained faint in my memory, blurred by time's passage.

The details of that event may have blurred with the years, but its festive resonance remained vivid, a joyous gathering that etched indelible impressions upon my soul. At that juncture, I was part of a group of young ladies united by the love of songs, and our harmonious voices often graced various gatherings. This particular occasion summoned us to perform, and we embraced the opportunity with boundless enthusiasm.

Amidst the lyrical sounds, my eyes alighted upon a tall, elegant figure, a guy whose complexion bore the rich hue of dark chocolate. He moved through the room with a quiet confidence that drew my gaze, and in that serendipitous moment, our eyes met, igniting a spark that defied explanation. I turned my head ever so slightly, driven by a curious blend of intrigue and fascination, our connection weaving an almost electric bond.

The performance unfurled, but as the melodies flowed, a pause was called, granting us a moment's respite. We were asked to take our seats briefly, and it was during this intermission that I noticed him rise from his chair, departing the room. Seizing the opportunity, I followed suit, slipping through the door mere moments after him.

Outside, I feigned a need for something, and as I ventured further, there he stood, engaged in conversation with another guest. As I drew nearer, he turned toward me, igniting a conversation with a simple, "How are you?" Though my concern at the time may have been minimal, I responded with politeness. Our exchange flowed with ease, and he introduced himself, leaving an indelible impression upon my heart.

We exchanged phone numbers, a simple act that would become the prelude to a chapter of significance in our lives. However, the stark reality remained that he resided in a city thousands of kilometers' away, bridging the distance through the rudimentary means of communication available at the time a far cry from the instantaneous connections we take for granted today, relying on sporadic emails and text-based messages.

Time meandered on, and eventually, I returned home from my extended sojourn during my boarding school tenure. It was on a tranquil Saturday, amidst the task of tidying my belongings from school, that I stumbled upon his phone number, a spark of recognition igniting within me. Excitement coursed through my veins as I seized the landline phone at home, my fingers trembling as I dialed his number. I waited with bated breath for him to answer the call, and when he finally did, his voice, rich with familiarity, greeted me with a warm, "Hey, my girl!" In that moment, a connection sparked to life once more.

As the scenes of life unfolded further, my mother discovered a series of calls on her landline, all from the same man with whom I had been conversing. Her reaction was one of fury, a response stemming from the fact that, as a young woman of that era, my exposure to the world's intricacies was limited. However, beneath her anger, life had woven its enchantment, for I had encountered someone with whom I could communicate openly, someone who listened to me.

Yet, there was an insurmountable geographical challenge, his residence in a distant city. To bridge the divide, I resorted to a clandestine routine, embarking on secret journeys to spend precious moments with him, concealed from the watchful eyes of my family. These covert trysts allowed us to savor stolen days together, a respite from the looming chasm of distance.

In those moments, the intensity of our emotions overshadowed all else, and the profound love we shared enveloped our thoughts. It was a love so all-consuming that we even contemplated the audacious notion of travelling to a foreign land together. But that happened at that early stage.

Coincidentally, an opportunity arose when a family member, residing abroad, extended an invitation for me to join her.

The prospect of such a significant move loomed before me, and as I contemplated the idea, I was gripped by a dilemma. How could I leave behind the love of my life for an entire month?

In the face of this decision, I chose to confront the reality of our connection. That night, I sat down with him for a heart-to-heart conversation, our words a testament to the depths of our love. We pondered the challenges that lay ahead how would we manage a relationship separated by thousands of kilometers? We revisited our past conversations and memories, delving into the emotions that had transpired.

We asked ourselves why those feelings existed and whether they were mutual. My heart raced incessantly, signaling that there was something special between us. I could see his heart beat through his chest. Despite the physical distance that stood as a barrier, we maintained our communication through phone calls.

Our love, however, seemed unyielding, and amidst our discussions, we arrived at a startling decision, a decision that would shape the course of our lives forever. We decided to bring forth a child together, believing it would bind us eternally. The days passed, the month arrived, and it brought with it a life-altering revelation.

In a society where such a decision was met with shock and disapproval, the news of my pregnancy sent shockwaves through my community. My mother, a woman deeply rooted in tradition and values, was filled with fear and anger. a young woman who was invested in the church made a drastic decision to be pregnant out of wedlock. She questioned my choices, wondering why I had allowed this to happen after all her teachings and protections. Yet, I remained resolute, for the decision we had made was one of mutual consent, born from the profound love that we both shared.

Returning home on that fateful day, I was overcome with a sense of sickness. My mother, recognizing the magnitude of the situation, took me into her care. She voiced her concerns, her disappointment palpable, but my heart remained steadfast.

The journey of my pregnancy unfolded, with him standing by my side, a constant presence in my life. My family knew him as the man responsible for my condition, and everything proceeded as smoothly as it could under the circumstances. He even proposed sending me to the US to have the baby, but my mother, her fears deep-seated, rejected the idea. She had already lost me once to a stepmother's torture, and the prospect of my travelling alone weighed heavily on her heart.

In the end, I stayed, choosing to face the challenges that lay ahead with unwavering resolve. My parents looked upon me as a disappointment, a label I wore with pride, for I knew the depth of love that had led me to this path. The pregnancy continued without incident, and my son, born from the crucible of our love, is now twenty-one years old, a memoir to the enduring power of our connection.

Though our union didn't culminate in marriage, the fear of my mother's domestic violence past was engraved in my spirit and marriage was the last thing on my mind. The complexities of family and societal expectations cast a shadow over our love story. He held deep respect for his family's wishes, and despite our intentions to chart our own course, their influence remained a significant factor in our lives. And so, our tale endures, a testament to the indomitable spirit of love that defied distance, time, and societal norms, a love that continues to define the course of our lives to this very day.

Chapter 5
CO-PARENTING

Our journey meandered through unexpected twists and turns, revealing a path uncharted and unpredictable. Marriage, it seemed, was a distant horizon, an elusive dream that fate had not destined for us. Instead, we embraced a different role that of co-parents, navigating the intricacies of raising our child together. Our dynamic was harmonious, our bond unbreakable, and life, for a time, found its equilibrium within our shared journey.

As the sands of time continued their relentless march, he encountered another presence, a woman with whom he glimpsed a future that bore the weight of matrimony. The notion of marriage sprouted anew, and he approached me with this newfound perspective. Naively, I entertained the thought, oblivious to the profound implications it would entail. At that juncture, marriage was a distant concept, tarnished by the shadows of my parents' tumultuous union. In my mind's eye, I envisioned our connection enduring, our friendship unwavering. I imagined us continuing to chat and confide in each other, our bond untouched by the formalities of marriage. Regrettably, my optimism would prove unfounded, and the departure of my closest friend was abrupt and jarring. It was then that the true gravity of marriage struck me a commitment that transformed the very essence of our relationship.

Our connection, once one of equals, shifted into the roles of father and mother. The realization hit me like a tidal wave, and tears flowed freely as I grappled with this new reality. In the days that followed, he tried to console me, imparting wisdom about the profound significance of marriage. It dawned on me that my initial understanding had been shallow, and slowly but surely, I began to fathom the weight of this solemn commitment.

I accepted that this was the path I needed to traverse, not for myself, but for the sake of our beloved child. Our journey as co-parents continued, a testament to our unwavering love and boundless kindness, guided by our shared faith. While our connection remained unbroken, new challenges emerged, particularly in other facets of our relationship as parents.

His bride appeared warm and welcoming towards my son, a façade often seen in the early stages of any relationship. However, as the pages of time turned, things became complicated, laying bare the faces of human nature. As I embarked on this new chapter of life, I faced the daunting decision of determining where our son would find his home. I chose to remain silent out of respect for their relationship, particularly due to the presence of a child born before their union. My primary focus was ensuring the well-being of our son, with a commitment not to emotionally disrupt his upbringing. This responsibility couldn't be shifted to anyone else, as it was a consensual decision between two adults to bring a child into the world.

Although he had spent time with my mother, I eventually chose to have him reside with his father, believing it would offer a more stable environment for him. My mother, in her ever-supportive role, alternated between caring for him and spending weekends together. The potential for a better life in various African countries, driven by his father's prospects for work, weighed heavily in this decision, a beacon of hope for a brighter future.

Yet, this decision came with its own set of challenges, chiefly revolving around communication with my mother and her perceptions of my role in the situation. It seemed his stepmom harbored feelings of abandonment, as if I had forsaken my child to embark on a personal journey. This barrier proved formidable, hindering any meaningful connection despite my earnest efforts to foster understanding and dialogue. Thus, I made the heart-wrenching choice to step back, observing how events would unfurl, all the while prioritizing the well-being of my child. Communication with his father remained our sole lifeline. Despite these hurdles, fate had more surprises in store.

Life took an unexpected turn when I crossed paths with someone who embraced both me and my son with open arms. Our connection flourished, blossoming over time until we made a pivotal decision to embark on a marital journey to the United States together.

However, this transition was not without its trials. Adapting to life in a foreign land presented its own set of challenges, compounded by the complex web of relationship dynamics. While the man in my life welcomed me and my child, it appeared that his mother was initially unaware of my son's presence.

This lack of awareness sowed discord and strained interactions, making my experience far from smooth and, at times, deeply distressing.

Chapter 6
TRANSITIONAL PARENTING

My life took an unexpected and tumultuous turn, transforming into a narrative filled with twists and formidable challenges. I was a vibrant and youthful woman in my early twenties, when destiny steered me towards the United States of America. My then husband, medical personnel navigating the complications of the healthcare system, had recently secured a position at a hospital in a different city. He resided at his sister's place, but embarked on weekly journeys to another city for work, a testament to his unwavering dedication to his burgeoning career.

As a newcomer to this vast and foreign land, my heart held dreams of establishing a loving home with the man I had longed for. Yet, reality had a different plan in store for me. Instead of a cozy abode with my husband, I found myself ensconced in his sister's home. This new chapter thrust me into the role of a surrogate maid, where I bore the responsibilities of cooking, cleaning, and providing unwavering support to her family.

As time ticked on, an opportunity emerged, one that would propel us from his sister's abode to his city of work. This transition promised not only a change in geography but also a fresh beginning in our journey as a couple. This relocation brought us closer to the epicenter of his medical career and opened new doors for our future together. However, beneath the surface of this promising change, unsettling feelings about him began to creep into my heart.

Despite these burgeoning doubts, my love for him eclipsed my reservations, and we embarked on this new chapter as husband and wife. Our time in this new city unfolded as a beautiful chapter in our love story. With my devoted husband and my son, we cultivated connections and built friendships within our community. Eventually, the profound step of marriage graced our lives, a momentous occasion that filled my heart with boundless joy.

As our love story continued to unfold, I had the immense blessing of carrying our second son in my womb. The anticipation of his arrival, the thought of holding his precious face in my arms, suffused my days with radiant light.

Yet, amid all this joy, the absence of my mother was keenly felt. A mother's support and guidance are treasures beyond measure, and I yearned for her presence and wisdom, especially as I embarked on this journey into motherhood alone. As a mother in a strange land, I longed for her by my side, for her nurturing presence to guide me through the challenges that lay ahead.

Upon bringing our precious baby home, my days became an unrelenting cycle of responsibilities. From the early hours of the morning, tending to my own needs, preparing nourishing meals, maintaining an orderly household, and managing myriad tasks, every aspect of life felt like an insurmountable feat.

The weight of these responsibilities rested solely on my shoulders, and it was an undoubtedly demanding and challenging period. Adding to the struggle, my then mother-in-law (may her soul rest in peace), firmly believed that I shouldn't expect her to fulfil the role my biological mother would have played. Thus, the monumental task of caring for our tiny infant fell squarely upon my inexperienced shoulders.

Nights became a mosaic of interrupted slumber, each one punctuated by waking up to attend to the baby's needs. I navigated this arduous journey mostly on my own, with my love and determination as my guiding lights.

This experience was both a relentless struggle and a

poignant reminder of what I had left behind in my home country. Back there, the extended family played a significant role in caring for and supporting a new mother. I recalled how my own mother and other family members shared the load, making the process more manageable. In contrast, here I was, halfway across the world, grappling with the formidable challenge of motherhood without the robust support network I had grown accustomed to.

While the absence of support weighed heavily on my heart, I was grateful that I didn't have to face postpartum challenges and pressures alone. Despite the unrelenting difficulties, I took proactive steps to better my situation. I enrolled myself in school, recognizing the importance of pursuing education even in the midst of these trials.

This journey transported me back to the time when I was pregnant, a time filled with expectations and uncertainties. The path I had chosen was undoubtedly tough, but my determination and resilience propelled me forward.

I enrolled in the university while heavily pregnant, embarking on a grueling daily commute. The drive to school consumed approximately an hour and twenty minutes each way. Despite the arduous journey, I was resolute in my commitment to attend classes and return home each day. Some days, exhaustion would overtake me, and I'd find myself parked on the side of the road, taking brief respites or even stealing precious moments for a nap.

After the birth of my baby, I faced the daunting reality of needing to place my cherished child in day-care. Each morning, I would drop him off, my heart heavy with the weight of leaving him in the care of strangers I had never met before. Tears often blurred my vision as I drove away, a poignant testament to the trials I was enduring.

Amidst these difficulties, I summoned strength and resilience, emerging as a better and stronger person. Navigating these trials shaped me in profound ways, forging a spirit that refused to yield. Friends came to my aid by preparing delicious meals, occasionally visiting to ensure I had the means to feed the baby properly.

However, as the pages of life continued to turn, its script took an even more tumultuous twist. My then-husband's family proved to be less of a support network, while my solitude became increasingly pronounced, overshadowed by mounting stress and the slow erosion of our marital bonds. This strained dynamic eventually led to our mutual decision to part ways. Blending two families might look easy but it's the most difficult family dynamics you can ever think of.

The divorce proceedings were arduous, and during this time, I found myself pregnant with our second child, my third son. Despite the complexities of our relationship, there were moments of beauty and love, though they often remained obscured by the weight of our significant issues. The divorce marked a decisive turning point. I was left to care for our three children, while he moved forward, remarried, and began a new chapter in his life. The process took its toll, and it was a year or two before he remarried. His new marriage and life continued on a different trajectory, while I navigated the formidable challenges of single motherhood.

These circumstances initially made it difficult for me to connect with the new relationship he had forged. My focus remained firmly on providing and nurturing our children, and the complexities of our situation tested my adaptability and resilience.

Anger, rage, and fear overwhelmed me as I grappled with the daunting prospect of managing life alone in a foreign land. I spent hours contemplating the extent of my suffering and questioning how much more I had to endure to improve my circumstances. I was conditioned to believe that I couldn't do anything without them, and that life would take a turn for the worse if I left. The fear of the unknown clouded my judgement. Despite the very real challenges, I confronted them with prayers and hard work. I questioned God, seeking answers for where I had gone wrong, but received none.

Chapter 7
BLENDED FAMILY DYNAMICS

As I ventured through this new phase of my life, I made a conscious decision to priorities my well-being and shield myself from the haunting specters of the past. Embracing my identity as a vibrant, young woman in a foreign land, I sought to reconstruct my life after the dissolution of a failed marriage.

During this transformative period, my ex-husband embarked on his own journey, one that led to a remarriage and the aspiration of a fresh start. However, the narrative of his new life took an unexpected turn, tainted by misunderstandings and the distortion of facts that clouded his new spouse's perception. The consequences were apparent when she visited, shrouded in a veil of defensiveness and hostility. Despite my inherent sociability, I couldn't help but detect the chill in her demeanor, prompting me to question the reasons behind her distant and unwelcoming behavior.

Nevertheless, I remained open to the prospect of building a connection with her. I understood the importance of fostering a bond, particularly in light of the agreement my ex-husband and I had crafted. We had agreed that I would have custody of our children during the school year, while he would have them during vacations aside from the court's decisions which were not favorable to both parties. It was paramount for me to cultivate a harmonious relationship with her, grounded in the unwavering belief that my children's upbringing should be characterized by consistency and nurturance.

My motivation was rooted in my maternal instinct, driven by the ardent desire to ensure support for my children, regardless of their whereabouts. I recognized that a united front between both households would provide the stability and guidance they required. Thus, I embarked on the arduous journey of building a connection with this woman, resolute in my determination to uncover common ground and shared values in our approach to parenting.

My endeavor was driven by the vision of creating a beautiful, cohesive and aligned environment for my children. Despite the inevitable challenges that surfaced along the way, my commitment to forging a collaborative partnership with their stepmom remained unwavering. I held the fervent hope that together, we could contribute to our children's growth, guaranteeing them a consistent wellspring of love, guidance, and a better upbringing, irrespective of the household they found themselves in.

As I navigated this very complicated path, I held fast to the conviction that my children's well-being, especially with their siblings and their comprehension of family bonds must forever remain at the forefront. Amidst these endeavors, my children's stepmother embarked on her own journey into motherhood, welcoming a daughter and then a son in quick succession, expanding our family tree.

With two households now woven into the fabric of our lives, the challenge lay in ensuring that my children could establish meaningful connections and unconditional love and friendship with their half-siblings. I was determined that they should internalize the profound lesson that even if their parents were no longer united, a united and loving family could still be cultivated across different homes. This objective became a driving force in my life.

Establishing a mutual relationship with my children's stepmother became a pivotal decision, one that opened doors to a level of better communication and collaboration surpassing even my exchanges with their father. Our fortified bond allowed us to coordinate attendance at our children's games and events, and we even ventured on joint vacations. Witnessing the genuine care and concerted effort we invested in nurturing this relationship for the sake of our children's happiness and well-being warmed my heart.

This family journey, though occasionally challenging, proved to be extraordinarily rewarding. Through Prayers, and unwavering commitment and shared values, we crafted a harmonious dynamic that enriched our children's lives. We've imparted in them the enduring power of love and unity, demonstrating that family bonds could thrive in the face of evolving circumstances. The experience was nothing short of remarkable, contributing a beautiful and heart-warming chapter to the story of our blended family.

Chapter 8
LOVE KNOWS NO BOUNDS

On another exquisite day, I find myself here, contemplating the myriad ways in which life might have unfolded with our cherished children. The depth of love and care we harbor for them is truly remarkable. As a young woman, raised within the warm embrace of a loving community, I've come to appreciate the profound significance of nurturing children and fostering the bonds that shape their lives.

My mother, a steadfast confidante and sage, bestowed upon me guidance that was as precious as it was invaluable. Despite being rejected from what should have been her home, she maintained a calm demeanor and built a relationship with my stepmother for the sake of our well-being and safety. Amidst all the painful stories I narrated to her from my bad experience with my stepmother, I found her giggling with her as friends just to secure a safe space for her kids. That character portrait is what I yearn for every day.

My mother has endured a lifetime in a blended family, where her father had children with another woman, introducing a source of ongoing pain and distraction. A once loving family dynamic transformed into one marred by competition and hatred, a reality of deep-seated animosity that persists to this day.

I've witnessed the manipulation of power, pride, disrespect, and discrimination from her own blood families. The unfortunate truth is that she fights daily to make her voice heard, but as a second-class citizen, her voice is often silenced. I've learned first-hand that forgiveness is a path to healing. Today, I am proud to see her assert her own voice and claim her rightful space.

In a world where many young women grapple with the absence of a strong support system, the prospect of venturing forth into life's trials loomed daunting. Often, I placed my own needs on the backburner, elevating the well-being of others above all else. The journey into motherhood at a tender age only served to bolster my determination.

I was resolute in my commitment to shield my children from the adversities that my mother had encountered during her youth. Consequently, I have often established clear boundaries and diligently instilled these cherished values into the lives of my beloved offspring. The wellspring of pride that swells within me as I bear witness to their remarkable growth into young men is immeasurable. My eldest son, aged twenty-two, stands as a testament to the enduring impact of my mother's wisdom. Following in his footsteps are my second son, aged sixteen, and the youngest at twelve. I have also gained a bonus son who is four, vibrant and smart awaiting to become a man as his step siblings. My blended family journey continues.

Nurturing them and witnessing the blossoming of their intelligence and integrity fills my heart with boundless joy. In a community where children often mirror the virtues and principles of their parents, I derive immense gratification from knowing that I've passed down the cherished values bequeathed to me by my own mother.

My journey through the corridors of a blended family has granted me the privilege of encountering an array of stories, shared by diverse families and friends. I've borne witness to their joys and endured alongside them during their struggles. It pains my heart to observe how relationships, once conceived from love and hope, can wither into something profoundly disheartening. The beautiful unions, where partners once regarded each other with love as the living embodiment of their dreams, sometimes take a grievous and unforeseen turn.

As I reflect upon these stories, I am profoundly grateful for the opportunity to listen and learn. I have come to realize, our lives are intricately woven with the threads of love and challenges, and I remain steadfast in my commitment to nurture my own family with the same unwavering care and devotion that my mother bestowed upon me. The bond that once captivated your attention and was meant to be the singular focus of your life can, regrettably, transform into a harrowing nightmare when a relationship falters, especially when a child is enmeshed within that toxic environment. Alas, many fails to recognize that even though a romantic relationship may conclude, the reverberations endure. A seed is sown, and as it matures, it may bear both beautiful blossoms and tainted fruits, irrespective of our preferences. Bearing a child with someone is a lifelong commitment, whether we consciously acknowledge it or not. It's as if a part of ourselves becomes forever entwined with that person, and relinquishing that connection feels akin to amputating a significant portion of our very being. We compromise, we protect, and we nurture another human being, shifting the axis of our desires from self-fulfillment to the welfare of the child we've brought into the world. It becomes an intrinsic facet of our existence, reshaping our priorities in ways we could never have anticipated.

Through my journey and experiences, I have come to understand that relationships, regardless of their initial promise, can take unforeseen twists and turns. Maturity has taught me that compromise is an essential ingredient for both survival and success. To thrive and prosper, we must sometimes yield. Building a robust relationship necessitates striking a delicate equilibrium where both parties contribute. It's not solely about one individual; at times, we must take into account the desires, needs, and preferences of the other person.

In the intricate dance of relationships and parenthood, finding common ground through compromise becomes not just important, but imperative. This is the foundation upon which we construct healthier, more gratifying connections, ensuring that the exquisite blossom of a child's life is nurtured within the fertile soil of a supportive and harmonious environment.

Chapter 9
HONORING INDIVIDUALITY

Waking up one beautiful morning, my reflection in the mirror was a stark reminder of the many swirling questions and doubts that had taken residence in my mind. Was I still the same person I once knew? or had the absence of the man with whom I had shared laughter and life altered me irrevocably? Dark thoughts of ending my own life flitted through my consciousness, but they remained just those thoughts, not a viable option. In the end, it wasn't even a consideration.

Amidst this tumultuous mental landscape, I contemplated the notion of leaving behind a brighter future for my children, the unwavering pillars of support in my life. They are everything to me, my reason to endure. And so, I made a solemn vow to release the negative thoughts that had ensnared me, embrace change, and painstakingly craft a more promising family life, fostering healthy relationships along the way.

It's worth remembering that what worked for me may not necessarily work for others. Every individual's journey is a unique experience, a personal voyage of self-discovery and transformation. Letting go became my guiding principle. I learned to set aside my ego, quell my pride, and relinquish frivolous attachments. Humility became my steadfast ally as I redirected my focus toward the well-being of my cherished children, their burgeoning futures, and even their father's role in their lives. After all, wasn't it in their best interest to have him in good health and actively present? His presence, I was certain, would invariably light up their lives with smiles and warmth.

Life, as I soon realized, demanded profound sacrifices as I navigated the tumultuous waters from a troubled relationship to a more prosperous and fulfilling one. In this transformation, I discovered that service to others ought to take precedence over self-interest. I resolved to be a provider, to support those around me, embracing the notion that I was meant to be a servant, not one who sought to be served.

One poignant memory stands out among the myriad moments that defined this transformative journey. It was the day my children were scheduled to travel to another city to reunite with their siblings. Arrangements had been made for their stepmother to pick them up from the airport. In an unexpected turn of events, this situation created a rare opportunity for candid conversation between us. Despite never having engaged in a proper dialogue about our relationships, this moment presented an opening, a chance for understanding to bloom. As we waited at the airport for the children's departure, their stepmother arrived earlier than expected. Originally planning to pick up the kids and return right back, flight delays compelled us to share a meal together.

Seated at a restaurant table, we found ourselves drawn into a conversation that delved far deeper than the immediate circumstances. It was a bonding experience, one that none of us had anticipated. When the waiter finally arrived with the bill, she offered reassurance, "Don't worry about it; I've got this. Trust me, I've got my husband's card." Laughter bubbled up from within us, and in that seemingly small gesture, a connection was forged, a connection based on understanding, camaraderie, and trust. This encounter proved instrumental in paving the way for a collaborative and trusting family dynamic, defying our initial apprehensions.

As time unfurled, our relationship continued to evolve. While there may have been reservations at the outset, I made a conscious choice to extend an olive branch, ensuring she felt comfortable and secure within the bounds of our newfound family. Today, my children lovingly refer to her as "mom," a title that hadn't come naturally in the beginning. In conclusion, my journey has been an odyssey marked by profound growth, unwavering sacrifice, and an unyielding commitment to nurturing relationships. By shedding the burden of negativity and embracing the mantle of humility, I have succeeded in building a stronger family unit founded upon mutual understanding, trust, and, above all, love.

Chapter 10
NAVIGATING COMPLEXITIES

As time flows steadily onward, our relationships continue to transform and evolve. When she first came to our lives, my children grappled with uncertainty, unsure of how to address her. I, too, faced the challenge of finding the right way to introduce her to my little ones. I often settled on the phrase, "Your second mom," as it provided a comforting and fitting description. Over time, my children adopted this term and began calling her "mom" as well.

This transition made sense, particularly because she had her own young children who naturally referred to her as "Mom." It would have been cumbersome and perhaps even awkward for my kids to address her differently when they visit her home. The term "Mom" seamlessly integrated into our situation, driven by both necessity and the warmth with which she welcomed my children. I believe this smooth transition in addressing her came about because she, too, was open and receptive to my children, embracing them wholeheartedly.

Yet, amid this harmonious integration, building a strong relationship with my first son's stepmother proved to be a more challenging endeavor. The reasons behind this difficult collaboration remain a mystery to me till date, shrouded in the complexities of our shared history.

As I cast my thoughts back to the past, a specific memory resurfaces a moment from nearly two decades ago. At the time, my first son was a mere toddler.

In a significant decision, I chose to entrust him to his father's care during my temporary absence, intentionally opting not to involve my mother in the matter. This decision, rooted in the belief that my child's father should shoulder his responsibilities and actively participate in his upbringing, did not elicit any objections from my mother. In essence, my aim was to foster a strong connection between my son and his father while also considering my mother's well-being and responsibilities. This choice underscored my conviction that the child's father should be an engaged parent, sparing my mother from bearing the sole burden, given that I had a partner who could share the parenting responsibilities.

The journey I've embarked upon has been one of growth, learning, and the intricate complexities in life and nurturing various relationships. Life has persistently conveyed the importance of humility, compromise, and a genuine willingness to understand others, all of which are pivotal in the creation of strong, lasting bonds. It extends beyond individual interests, focusing instead on the greater good of a harmonious family unit that has thrived through success, love, understanding, and collaborative efforts.

Nevertheless, my mother didn't readily accept the notion of my child being entrusted to his father, particularly since we were not married at the time. This child was, after all, her grandchild, and she believed that his life was incomplete without the presence of a father figure. I navigated this sensitive situation delicately, assuring my mother that I harbored no intention of burdening her with the responsibility of my child while his dad is alive.

Mothers, as I have come to observe, tend to priorities their child's well-being above all else. They can also be fiercely protective at times, a quality that can sometimes manifest as hesitation or overprotection. My own mother, in particular, had an exceptionally strong protective streak, perhaps rooted in her past relationship trauma. This protective nature led her to be cautious of allowing anyone into her circle. Forming bonds with new individuals, especially in the light of her past misunderstandings with some family members, is a challenging endeavor. While I empathized with her perspective, it did create a certain degree of tension within our family dynamics.

As I became more deeply involved in these intricate relationships, I made every effort to bridge the gap and establish a connection with my son's stepmother. Unfortunately, it became evident that a barrier had already been erected, one founded on prior conflicts with my mother. I sympathized with the challenges she faced and the reservations she harbored about welcoming me into her world. I extended multiple olive branches in an attempt to initiate a connection, but everyone, it seemed, carried their own unique struggles and battles in life. Building relationships, I learned, was often the most formidable part of life's journey.

Reflecting on my experiences, I take solace in the fact that I maintained a certain level of respect and restraint. Even in the face of the opportunity to pursue a relationship with her husband, I recognized and respected the boundaries that were firmly in place. My unwavering commitment to my values and principles served as a guiding light, preventing me from crossing any lines that could have compromised the delicate balance of our complex family dynamics. In the end, I am profoundly grateful for the precious gifts I have received, my children who have enriched my life beyond measure.

Many individuals encounter formidable challenges when it comes to navigating the complex terrain of blended families and relationships. It is a journey fraught with ups and downs, one that requires steadfast determination. Yet, it is essential that we all take a moment to sit down and earnestly evaluate what truly matters. We must recognize that the children we are raising together are not solely ours; it took two people to bring them into this world. It is high time we break down the walls that divide us, cultivate forgiveness within ourselves, and work tirelessly to foster healthier relationships with our ex-partners while respecting boundaries. Through understanding, compassion, and relentless effort, we can pave the way for a more harmonious and brighter future for all.

Chapter 11
A LASTING LEGACY

The voyage through the complication of pain and challenges within a blended family has etched profound lessons into my life's canvas. This journey led me to a pivotal crossroads - a moment of revelation where I chose to shed all pretenses and embrace the authenticity of my being. This authenticity became the guiding light for my interactions with my beloved children. My overarching aspiration: to immerse myself in life's rich scenery of experiences and dreams, all while cradling a hopeful prayer in the depths of my heart. Above all, our ceaseless efforts are intricately woven into the fabric of crafting a brighter future, one that bestows upon our cherished children lives enriched with love, resilience, and the harmonious union of our blended family.

In the crucible of a blended relationship, I unearthed profound lessons that have irrevocably transformed me into a more compassionate, understanding, and resilient soul. The crucible of blended love has imparted wisdom that transcends the boundaries of forgiveness, love, and the profound significance of unity. It has humbled me, teaching me that no matter the vigor of one's efforts, the souls entwined in the intricate dance of relationships must be open and willing to extend their arms in welcoming embrace.

Today, I wish to extend my gratitude and appreciation towards my ex-husband and his beloved wife for their instrumental roles in nurturing our shared children. Together, we've created an environment of love and peace, resolutely resisting attempts to paint a different, discordant picture. While the world may have misconceptions, we, as co-parents, have attuned our focus to a singular and unwavering truth: the happiness of our children stands paramount.

In the crucible of our family bonds, we've forged a system that caters to the needs of both households, creating an environment where our children eagerly anticipate the joys of their shared moments. They've grown to perceive one another not as mere individuals but as siblings, bound by the unbreakable thread of shared paternal DNA.

What has proven efficacious for me in this relationship is the delicate art of respect and non-interference. Success blossomed as I breathed life back into sensitivity, considering the collective picture of past experiences that wove us together before the present. This choice granted me the freedom from the shackles of emotional turmoil and fostered an environment of tranquility. It's crucial to understand that there exists no universal formula for the perfect relationship. What works for one may not work for another; reality beckons us towards the path of acceptance and onward progression.

People enter our lives for myriad reasons, each bearing a unique gift. Some bestow the promise of a shared future, while others grace us with the gift of progeny. Some sprinkle the magic of happiness, while others may momentarily cloud our skies with sorrow. Yet, in the grand expression of existence, what truly matters is our ability to accept and reciprocate the offerings of those who traverse our path.

Being an integral part of a blended family has revealed to me that even amidst the murk of hurt and uncertainty, the possibility of nurturing joy, contentment, and unity is very much within reach. Hate and bitterness often shroud the light of reason when relationships crumble. However, it is vital to remember that the conclusion of a partnership does not diminish one's intrinsic worth. It simply signifies the recognition that something different and perhaps better awaits. The cessation of a relationship does not define your essence; it merely signifies a shift in the tides of destiny.

In my present journey within another Blended Family scenario, my betrothed husband brings along a son whom I'm yet to meet. Engaging in a heartfelt conversation with him, I felt the wellspring of love within me, a love capable of stretching its arms to embrace this new addition. He too is a result of A Blended Family. This experience evoked a unique sentiment, a sentiment navigated with a profound understanding of what it truly means to be part of a Blended Family. What has worked for me may not be universally applicable. Thus, the question lingers: will others be receptive enough to acknowledge that this little boy shares bonds with his half-siblings, bonds that have the potential to bloom into a shared life?

As for me, I harbor no apprehensions, for my heart overflows with an abundance of love.

This beautiful journey through the complications of blended families has not been devoid of its lessons. It has ushered me toward self-discovery, guiding me toward the practice of releasing emotional entanglements and shedding the shackles of negativity. Detaching from the weighty burden of anger, hatred, and bitterness has been a liberating experience. This liberation has paved the way for my progress and personal growth.

Blended families, especially within the cultural context of African societies, often bear the heavy yoke of societal misconceptions and stereotypes. However, my journey has shown me that by detaching from preconceived notions, societal pressures, and the baggage of emotions, we can forge a path toward harmony and unity.

I acknowledge the myriad challenges that accompany the territory of blended families, for I have personally traversed the path of pain and confusion they entail. The preconception that blended families are destined for discord and strife is far from universal. My own experiences serve as a testament to the transformative power of releasing negativity and embracing forgiveness, offering the opportunity to rewrite the narrative.

My story carries with it hope that through the prism of my experiences, others may glean insights and discover their own pathways to healing and reconciliation. It is imperative to remember that there exists no singular formula for success within the realm of blended families. However, my fervent aspiration is that my journey may serve as a beacon of light, illuminating the path for others to embark on their own journeys toward solace, forgiveness, and renewed purpose within their blended family dynamics.

In a world often marred by resentment and conflict, I harbor an unyielding belief that by embracing the principles of detachment, forgiveness, and empathy, blended families can rise as exemplars of unity and love. Together, we can redefine the narrative, rewriting the story of familial bonds and shaping a world that thrives on love and understanding. My journey is a testament to the boundless power of resilience, hope, and the enduring potential for positive change. To all those navigating the complicated paths of blended families, I extend my love, support, and unwavering encouragement to you.

Chapter 12
WHAT'S TO THRIVE

Blending two families into one takes effort. Stepparents may feel resented. Step-siblings may feel unheard and disregarded. Various family members may feel that there is inherent bias and that certain family members are favored over others. Building new relationships can be painful. It takes time, communication, a thick skin, among other qualities to form a functional and healthy blended family.

Sometimes a stepparent may feel ignored by their stepchildren. But a stepchild is handling an array of ill feelings about his new life. Most of all, there is real guilt about not being with both his parents, and he feels a certain loyalty to the parent not present. Expect them to feel sad and moody. A good relationship with a stepchild cannot be forced, you can't make people want what you want.

You cannot force a child to love or even like a new stepparent. But it helps if the new parent and stepchild find common likes and dislikes. Is there a movie, show, book, or music that they are all interested in? Mutual ground will help family members feel included and not like complete strangers.

This has worked for me in many ways. Incorporating both

families whether far or new helps create long lasting bonds that cannot be broken. Children trust very easily and you want to be sensitive with that as you create bonds and memories with your step kids.

Parenting and family relationships can come with all sorts of challenges, and blended families are no different. Some of the unique challenges that those who form this type of family may face can be difficult, but their experiences can also be highly rewarding. If you're part of or considering forming a blended family, these tips we discussed here could help you set yourself and each member up for success.

Each family's situation is different. That said, there are some general strategies you might consider that could help the members of your blended family feel seen and cared for and to smooth the transition of combining households and or family time.

1. Give it time

Combining families especially if this entails combining households can feel a bit chaotic at first, in some cases. It can take time for the members to adjust logistically, emotionally, and in other ways, so patience and compassion along the way are generally key. The American Academy of Child and Adolescent Psychiatry suggests that it often takes between one and two years for blended families to adjust to the new situation. While this can seem like a long time if you're just starting out in this process, know that you're likely to see positive progress and milestones along the way. Staying consistent, being mindful of the changing needs of the child(ren) involved, and reminding them that they are loved and listened to can all be especially helpful during this period.

2. Provide structure

Children can be very adaptable and resilient in the right environments. To provide them with the support they need as your family transitions, it's often helpful to ensure that there is structure and routines in place. Consistent bedtimes, chores and responsibilities, regular family bonding time, and a stable living environment are all examples of these that you and your partner can set up in order to benefit the children you are now raising together. As they adjust to all the changes in their lives, these predictable structures can help them feel grounded. Plus, routines can benefit kids over the longer term, too. For example, research suggests that children who have a consistent and early bedtime may experience improved sleep, increased emotional stability and language development, healthy parental attachment, and other potential benefits.

3. Remain flexible

Although structure is important, sticking to it too rigidly and not allowing for feedback and changes can cause problems. Sometimes, the way you originally envisioned some element of your blended family's life might not end up being realistic. Leaving room for changes in plans and new feelings that may arise can be helpful.

For example, putting too strong an emphasis on bonding time as a family right away might be too m u c h f o r some children, especially adolescents and/or those who are having an especially difficult time with the transition. So even though you may have imagined engaging in this type of close family time every other night, adjusting your expectations to give the children a bit more space at first could go a long way towards easing the transition over the longer term.

1. Manage relationships with exes

If both partners are bringing children from previous relationships into a new blended family, there's the potential for two ex-partners to continue being involved in their lives. Those who have custody agreements with co-parents in the same area may have to interact with their ex and/or their partner's ex frequently. Doing your best to keep these relationships cordial, stable, and calm will typically benefit the children and help avoid conflict.

2. Keep the lines of communication open

The value of communication is often emphasized when discussing relationships of all kinds, including blended family relationships. Setting aside time to regularly check in and communicate about how things are going can ensure all members have the chance to say their feelings, frustrations, suggestions, and requests about the new family dynamic. Making sure everyone feels comfortable saying and understanding that their opinions are valued can also help. This could be achieved by teaching children about what it means to practice active listening, setting rules related to respect, honesty, interrupting, etc. when someone else is talking, and inviting everyone to set and communicate their own boundaries as needed.

TAKE HOME MESSAGE

When you and a new partner choose to combine your families, you have the chance to create new traditions, memories, and connections as a new blended unit. It is natural, however, to experience challenges along the way. Some strategies for helping manage the transition could include creating structure for your children, keeping lines of communication open, and remaining flexible as needed. If you need additional support, you might consider talking with a therapist who specializes in families and relationships.

Reference: *BetterHelp.com**

THE END

ABOUT THE AUTHOR

Germaine Kang (Roy Mamah)

RN, BSN, MSN | Talk Show Host | Matchmaker

|Relationship Coach | Mental Health Advocate

| Philanthropist | CEO

Germaine Kang, known as Roy Mamah, is a versatile professional who has excelled in multiple domains, seamlessly combining my expertise as a Nurse with my roles as a social media personality, talk show host, matchmaker, Mayo clinic advocate relationship coach, philanthropist, CEO, mental health advocate and many more. With a substantial and engaged online following, I have bridged the gap between healthcare professionalism and relatable influencer status.

My life journey is a testament to resilience and empowerment, characterized by my ability to overcome significant challenges. I faced a mental health crisis stemming from societal judgments surrounding my experience as a single mother, followed by the complexities of raising children after a broken marriage. These adversities propelled me towards a profound transformation, igniting my passion to assist others in navigating similar struggles.

Today, I stand as a beacon of hope and strength in my community and beyond. As a dedicated registered nurse, accomplished author, and dynamic talk show host, I leverage my platform to destigmatize mental health issues and advocate for holistic healing. My influence extends far beyond the healthcare industry, inspiring thousands to embrace their unique stories and confront their own mental health challenges with authenticity and vulnerability.

My multifaceted journey also paved the way for me to become a compassionate, talk show host and a matchmaker. Drawing upon my personal insights, I guide individuals toward establishing healthy and meaningful connections. My life's mission revolves around uplifting others, demonstrating that every obstacle can serve as a stepping stone to personal and professional greatness.

Roy Mamah, with her diverse skills and unwavering commitment to promoting others well-being, continues to make a profound impact on the lives of those she touches, embodying the essence of resilience, empowerment, and compassion. find below our services.

ROY MAMAH CONSULTING LLC

HOME CARE SERVICES

At **Granny Christy Home Care**, our team of skilled and dedicated caregivers, nurses, and therapists are specially trained to cater to the unique needs of each individual. We offer a comprehensive range of services, including personal care, medication management, companionship, and specialized therapies.

MENTAL HEALTH SOLUTIONS

Our team of experienced and licensed mental health professionals, including psychiatrists, psychologists, counsellors, and therapists, are committed to providing personalized treatment plans tailored to each individual's unique needs.

RELATIONSHIP COACHING

Our Relationship Coaching service is designed to help individuals and couples build healthier and more fulfilling connections in their personal and romantic relationships. Through tailored coaching sessions, clients gain valuable insights into their relationship dynamics, learn effective conflict resolution techniques, and develop skills to foster trust, respect, and understanding.

PERSONAL DEVELOPMENT

Our Personal Development service is a transformative journey that empowers individuals to unlock their full potential and achieve personal growth and self-improvement. Through personalized coaching and guidance, our team of dedicated professionals assists clients in identifying their strengths, setting meaningful goals, and overcoming obstacles that may hinder progress.

TALK SHOWS

Our talk shows *(The Roy Mamah Show, Undisclosed, Sunday Fun day, Match-Making Show)* are dynamic platforms that ignite engaging and thought-provoking conversations on a wide range of topics, from current affairs and social issues to entertainment, personal growth and secrets shared.

ROY MAMAH FOUNDATION INC

The Roy Mamah Foundation & Support Group are pillars of compassion in the community, dedicated to making a positive impact on the lives of those in need. Through our charitable initiatives, we extend a helping hand to various vulnerable populations, including the underprivileged, marginalized, and those facing challenging circumstances.

Visit us at; www.roymamahconsulting.com

Made in the USA
Columbia, SC
04 February 2025

53313914R00052